AFFINITY AND KINDRED

Lives shaped by sea and faith

First published in Great Britain 2015 by Jumbo Editions

Designed by Phil Gray at gris.gris   http://philgray.info/

The typefaces used in this book are Adobe Jenson Pro and Gill Sans. Nicolas Jenson was one of the finest printers working in Venice during the Incunabula period of the 1470s and his type is characteristically Humanist, a description that has also been given to Eric Gill's sans serif of 1928.

ISBN 978-0-9566264-6-2

All images from this book may be purchased as limited edition prints from:
www.affinityandkindred.com/contact.html

This copy is number 121   in a limited edition of 500

Thanks to:

WRITERS'
CENTRE
NORWICH

—— National Centre *for* Writing ——

AFFINITY AND KINDRED

Lives shaped by sea and faith

RICHARD DENYER

Photographs made in Norfolk and the Western Isles

Words by David Matless and Will Self

Hamarsaigh, Scalpay. Isle of Harris

Preface

When I first visited the Outer Hebrides in 2012, I was surprised to discover an immediate sense of connection between the islands and my home county of Norfolk. To begin with, this connection resided in contrasting extremes in land/water relationships, a preoccupation of my photographic work for many years, and for the moment it was enough to reflect that in the Norfolk Broads and northern Holland where I had previously worked, I was looking at water surrounded by land and in the Hebrides I was looking at land surrounded by water.

As I re-visited familiar locations in Norfolk and gradually became acquainted with the landscapes and residents of Harris, Lewis and then the southern islands of the Hebridean archipelago, I was drawn more and more towards photographing people with reference to their working lives and their relationship with the contrasting landscapes. In Hebridean communities I was particularly attracted to sites of vocation and devotion, especially the interiors of boat yards and churches. Thus the connection with Norfolk began to take shape. Beyond their generalised appeal I'm not particularly interested in the exteriors of these buildings. I *am* interested in how they are used: where the furniture is placed, how the implements of service and communion are organised in churches; how tools are arranged in craft workshops where hierarchies of utility are sometimes more obvious – a hammer immediately at hand, a specialised cutting tool in a store cupboard.

The county of Norfolk and the islands of the Outer Hebrides can be similarly distinguished by the sheer number of churches and the historic importance of boat building and repair yards. Few members of the older communities remain untouched by sea or faith, often both. Such affinities represent ideas and habits once considered immutable but which now struggle against a progressively mechanised and secular society, making these sites increasingly anachronistic. These visual legacies of disappearing ways of life might now appear incomprehensible to outsiders or those of a younger generation. In *Landmarks* (2015), when considering the loss of native language, Robert Macfarlane writes: *'It is not, on the whole, that natural phenomena and entities themselves are disappearing; rather that there are fewer people able to name them, and that once they go unnamed they go to some degree unseen'*. In his introduction to *Affinity and Kindred*, David Matless refers to an unfamiliarity with common names for nautical and ecclesiastic objects in boat yards and churches. Perhaps I could visualise the ebbing tide of connections between ideas, materials and indigenous knowledge contained in these singular spaces.

The closest I have to a photographic hero, Walker Evans, believed in the revelations of the environment. In *Walker Evans: The Hungry Eye*, (Thames and Hudson, 1993), Gilles Mora and John T. Hill describe how Evans saw that the placing of objects in a domestic or working interior might reveal more about the character and psychology of the owner than including that person in the photograph. (Evans held similarly distinctive opinions about the inherent shortcomings of photographic portraiture, given that photography is a matter of surfaces. I empathise with these views, and would only observe that with regard to my own photographs, context is everything.)

A glance at the shelves of bookshops and tourist offices in Norfolk and the Outer Hebrides confirms the preponderance of photo-laden volumes dedicated to landscapes rendered dramatic through artful composition and meteorological extremes. Such picturesque scenes remain seductive and hard for a photographer to resist but often add little to the reader's knowledge of place and condition. In contrast, Walker Evans often used sequential rather than summary images, providing an invaluable counterpoint to the perpetual search for Henri Cartier-Bresson's elusive decisive moments of photographic exposure around which so much mythology has been created. In this photographic essay my approach is to offer careful pairings of images in which narrative links between my chosen locations and subjects are described. Some of these links will be clear, some less so, although I hope the pictures reward repeated viewings. The single larger images are included to provide wider descriptive contexts of space and place.

On the long drive home from my first visit to the Hebrides I began to work out connections between the landscape and culture I had just experienced and photographs previously made for *Still Waters* (1998) and *Neither Land nor Water* (2011) in Norfolk and northern Holland respectively. The phrase *Affinity and Kindred* neatly characterises these connections. The title is appropriated from the Church of England's 'Table of Kindred and Affinity' included in the Book of Common Prayer published since 1662, '*wherein whosoever are related are forbidden by the Church to marry together*'. Unsurprisingly the two lists are headed Mother and Father, a tenuous reference in my case to autobiographical themes which underpin many of the photographs.

Selecting from hundreds of images for this book was a nightmare, I should really have left it to others – advice I offer students but rarely apply to myself. There are so many balances to achieve between subject matter, location, tonality, colour and composition, and that's before considering each image's ability to convey individual or collective meaning. (The images show the full frame, no cropping or PhotoShop tricks.) There is no beginning, middle or end to the set of photographs. They can be viewed in any order. It is not my intention to provide answers but rather to purposefully articulate questions.

I hope you enjoy the book.

Richard Denyer, 2015

Vessels and Smiles - David Matless

In *Affinity and Kindred* Richard Denyer gives a comparative excursion to places shaped by water. Photographs are taken on journeys close to home, within 25 miles or so of Denyer's central Norfolk base, and during stays further afield in the Outer Hebrides. Occasional broad prospect scenes interject into sequences showing craft interiors, ritual rooms, and images of workaday and domestic devotion. Workshops, churches, chapels, beaches and living rooms give Denyer occasion to look, and to picture.

Affinity and Kindred extends photographic styles and topics found in Denyer's earlier collections. The 1989 publication *Still Waters* presented black and white photographs of the Norfolk and Suffolk Broads, images of buildings and waterways, with field portraits of people whose livelihoods and pleasures revolved around rivers and boats. The craft of boat restoration, for employment or hobby, was a running theme, as it remains in *Affinity and Kindred*, though in the current collection the Norfolk focus goes beyond Broadland to encompass the county's coast and agricultural interior. Denyer's Broadland work developed in commissions for the Broads Authority, the planning authority for the region, which in 1989 was granted national park status[2]. Denyer recalls acting as Authority photographer for dignitary visits; the Prince of Wales sailing an historic wherry, Margaret Thatcher swatting away a swallowtail butterfly attracted by her bright lapel.

Restoration work, Upton, Norfolk Broads

In 2002 Denyer provided colour photographs for the official national park guide to the region, accompanying text by Clive Tully[3]. While Denyer's commissioned work

---

1 Richard Denyer, *Still Waters: Photographs of the Norfolk and Suffolk Broads* (Still Waters Press, 1989)

2 David Matless, *In the Nature of Landscape: Cultural Geography on the Norfolk Broads* (Wiley-Blackwell, 2014)

3 Clive Tully and Richard Denyer, *The Broads: the Official National Park Guide* (Pevensey Press, 2002)

River Yare at Cantley sugar beet factory, Norfolk

Denyer revisited Broadland in a comparative exhibition at Norwich Arts Centre in February-March 2012, *Neither Land nor Water*, showing images of 'water, land and sky in Broadland and the Netherlands'. Photographs of Broadland and Friesland mixed, the regions presented in mutual recognition through lives led by water; boating pleasures and waterside

illustrated the Broads Authority's narrative of regional landscape heritage and value, keeping within particular aesthetic bounds, *Still Waters* stretched regional visual culture. Denyer could happily picture conventionally idyllic scenes, yet also showed an eye for objects generally cut out of any celebration of what the Broads Authority then labelled the 'last enchanted land'; plain bungalows, garden bird topiary, sugarbeet piles, old tyres. *Still Waters'* cover image reflected this pluralist aesthetic, showing Cantley's riverside sugar beet processing plant, the factory plume blending with clouds, and both reflected in the river. A coot attempts running take-off across the Yare, helping gather the factory into the scene.

dwelling, landscapes of drainage and threatened flood, wetland ecologies shaped by or defended against human construction. *Neither Land nor Water* showed tripod-shot, long exposure colour images, structures standing sharp while water and sky sometimes moved into blur. Dutch neatness sat alongside more ragged-edged England, tidy canal sides against makeshift riverbanks, with Friesland happily accommodating a waterside industrial and residential modernism. Only Cantley's factory appeared structurally so bold in Broadland. The display of Broadland and Friesland together served to variegate Broadland in comparison; bespoke gardened riverbank neatness shying from the modern, roughly unready shacks and moorings tattily content, the 19th century

Yare-Waveney 'New Cut' straight as a Zuiderzee causeway.

Affinity and Kindred extends Denyer's regional comparative method, and re-treads, as in *Still Waters*, some earlier photographic footsteps. Photographing Broadland in the late 20th century, Denyer worked in a region 'discovered' for leisure in the late 19th century in part by photographers. While John Payne Jennings and George Christopher Davies are now recalled primarily for illustrative work for guidebooks and railway companies, one Broadland photographer

postcard reproduction, a key reference point in establishing an historic visual grammar of Broadland landscape[4]. Denyer's documentation took up Broadland a century on from Emerson,

New Cut, Haddiscoe Island, Norfolk

Afsluitdijk causeway, Zuiderzee, northern Holland

though the figures in his landscape feature as named individuals, even self-conscious waterside characters, rather than Emerson's unnamed reed-cutting peasant social types. Setting Denyer's

has a prominent place in the history of art photography. The work of Peter Henry Emerson presented, as the title of his key 1886 work (with painter Thomas Goodall) put it, *Life and Landscape on the Norfolk Broads*. Emerson was subject to rediscovery from the mid-20th century as a pioneer of photographic modernism, and in the late 20th century became, through exhibitions and

work alongside Emerson highlights how naming, or not

4 Neil McWilliam and Veronica Sekules (eds) *Life and Landscape: PH Emerson, Art and Photography in East Anglia 1885-1900* (Sainsbury Centre for Visual Arts, 1986); Cliff Middleton, *The Broadland Photographers* (Albion, 1978); John Taylor, *The Old Order and the New: PH Emerson and Photography 1885-1895* (Prestel, 2006)

naming subjects, leads individuals to stand for a place in different ways, with possibilities and constraints either way. Are individuals to be reduced to types? Are regions to be reduced to characters?

Moving in *Affinity and Kindred* to the Hebrides, Denyer finds himself in other photographic footsteps, and marks his path with an opening quote from Walker Evans: 'If the thing is there, why there it is!' The American documentary photographic tradition shaped by Evans informs Denyer's images of vernacular clarity, with their attention to commonplace shapes and daily form. And if the thing is there, then others may of course have been there before to take pictures; both regions in *Affinity and Kindred* are trodden photographic ground. Since his 1979 book *The Hebrides*[5], Gus Wylie, a friend of Denyer and fellow photographer of Broadland working, as one of his projects put it, 'In the Shadow of Emerson', has documented Scottish island life and landscape. The Hebrides also register in the international art photographic canon through Paul Strand's 1962 book *Tir*

A'Mhurain: *The Outer Hebrides of Scotland*, with text by Basil Davidson. Strand's romantic socialist take on island folklore and livelihood mixes landscape prospects, details of rock, building, boats, grass, and portraits of named individuals[6].

The faces in Strand's portraits, as in Evans', or in Emerson's working scenes, tend to the serious, with concentration on the shown full face. Denyer's portraits – colour here, black and white in *Still Waters* – often show smiles. The subject's awareness of the photographer, their pose for the camera, here offers relaxed demeanour. Rachel and Donald MacSween, pictured in their Scalpay home, beam. The impression is of photography as companionable interaction, rather than dutiful pose for a higher purpose. Free churchmen begin to crack a smile, and, were we to see the faces on the headless array of Walsingham clerics, they might be pictured grinning to be on pilgrimage. The photographer, as ever, marks the image, and there is an ease of practice here, in keeping with Denyer's companionable persona. If the lives of photographer and subject are very different, affinities may be found, and exchange opened. The religious subjects of this collection may also indicate another form of exchange, between Denyer's younger self, raised in a clerical household, and the present adult atheist retaining affinity with the spaces of worship, older man and younger boy still kindred.

The photographic pairings in *Affinity and Kindred* are not always comprised of one image from each place;

_____

5 Gus Wylie, *The Hebrides* (Collins, 1979); Martin Padget, *Photographers of the Western Isles* (John Donald, 2010)

6 Paul Strand, *Tir A'Mhurain: The Outer Hebrides of Scotland* (Aperture, 2002; first published as Paul Strand and Basil Davidson, *Tir A'Mhurain / Outer Hebrides* [MacGibbon and Kee, 1962]); Fraser MacDonald, *Paul Strand and the Atlanticist Cold War*, History of Photography 28 (4) 2004, 357-374

pairing conveys affinities and kinships which are variously geographical, gestural, formal. Shapes converse; tables and altars, sills and alcoves, drapes and covers, towel ring and net tie, pipework and shrine. A recurrent form is the vessel, whether boat or otherwise, indeed the collection is shaped by forms to hold and catch things. Some are tricky to name without the requisite nautical or ecclesiastical language; the curved tube in the Stiffkey boatyard, the urn-like object topped with a cross in Vatersay church. Looking through the images, forms for holding include: bin, bottle, bowl, box (cardboard, metal, plastic, wooden), bucket, cabinet, can, candleholder, canister, chalice, crow's nest, cup, drawer, hands, jar, jug, kettle, net, niche, pipe, pot, receptacle, shell, shrine, sink, tray, tub, urn, vase.

Norfolk and the Hebrides carry expansive qualities; the North Sea from Salthouse Heath's relative height, the waving Minch waters, large beaches and boulders, big sky. The prevailing scale in these photographs though is small, contained, close. The outside is made miniature in modelled boats, while table tops make their own miniature landscapes, the objects of craft and ritual in arrangement. A boat even forms an altar in Eriskay church. Should we then regard this collection as a study of the altars of craft? A meditation on physical and spiritual labours in parallel? Perhaps, but any sombre and dutiful study of worship and workshop is neatly deflected by a fascination for adjacent spaces and their accoutrements; calendars, hooks, cupboards, kettles, curtains. In church, Denyer photographs where vicars wash their hands,

before or after the main business. An eye for idiosyncrasy, and for objects out of the way, moves these images beyond predictable registers of craft and devotion. Other things enter in; urns for tea, fluid for cleansing, towels for wiping, electrics by the virgin.

Nottingham, 2015

If the thing is there, why there it is!

Walker Evans

Our Lady St. Mary, South Creake, Norfolk

International Boatbuilding Training College, Lowestoft, Suffolk

Calum MacSween, Ardinashaig, Scalpay, Isle of Harris

Ken Tidd, north Norfolk

Hushinish, Isle of Harris

Calum MacSween's dry stone walling, Scalpay, Isle of Harris

Wassail procession, Elsing, Norfolk

St. Margaret's, Tatterford, Norfolk

David Hewitt's boatyard, Stiffkey, Norfolk

Tom Gathercole and David Hewitt, Stiffkey, Norfolk

Rachel and Donald MacSween, Scalpay, Isle of Harris

Empty church, South Uist

Weybourne, north Norfolk coast

The Minch

Neal Thompson's boatyard, Glandford, Norfolk

Our Lady St. Mary, South Creake, Norfolk

Henry Fillery's boatyard, Coldham Hall, Norfolk Broads

Unnamed church, Norfolk

Our Lady of Sorrows Roman Catholic church, Garrynamonie, South Uist

Hewitt's boatyard, Stiffkey, Norfolk

Outend Road croft, Scalpay, Isle of Harris

Wherry Yacht Charter, Wroxham, Norfolk Broads

High Street shop, Walsingham, Norfolk

Brillo and Ivor, Marine Harvest Salmon Farm, East Loch Tarbert, Isle of Harris

Melody and Estelle sorting mussels, Brancaster, north Norfolk

Net Services plant room, Scalpay, Isle of Harris

Shrine of Our Lady of Walsingham, Norfolk

St. Nicholas, Salthouse, Norfolk

St. Mary the Virgin, Titchwell, Norfolk

St. Ayles Skiff workshop, Castlebay, Barra

Steve Dilworth, sculptor, Geocrab, South Harris

Donald MacSween, Scalpay, Isle of Harris

Herring gutting shed, Scalpay, Isle of Harris

Crab boat, 'The Auk', David Hewitt's boatyard, Stiffkey, Norfolk

Marine Harvest Salmon Farm,
East Loch Tarbert, Isle of Harris

41

David Hewitt's boatyard, Stiffkey, Norfolk

St. Margaret's, Cley, Norfolk

St. Mary the Virgin, Elsing, Norfolk

International Boatbuilding Training College, Lowestoft, Suffolk

David Hewitt's boatyard, Stiffkey, Norfolk

Deacon's Court, Free Church, Scalpay, Isle of Harris

The Clisham, Isle of Harris

Net Services, Scalpay, Isle of Harris

Free Presbyterian church, Stokinish, South Harris

Priory Church of All Saints, Weybourne, Norfolk

St. Ayles Skiff, Ian Duffill's boatyard, Thurning, Norfolk

Holiday cottage, Scalpay, Isle of Harris

St. Michael's Roman Catholic church, Eriskay, South Uist

St. Margaret's, Cley, Norfolk

St. Michael's Roman Catholic church, Eriskay, South Uist

International Boatbuilding Training College, Lowestoft, Suffolk

St. John's, Stiffkey, Norfolk

St. Joseph's Roman Catholic church, Howbeg, South Uist

Hemsby, Norfolk coast

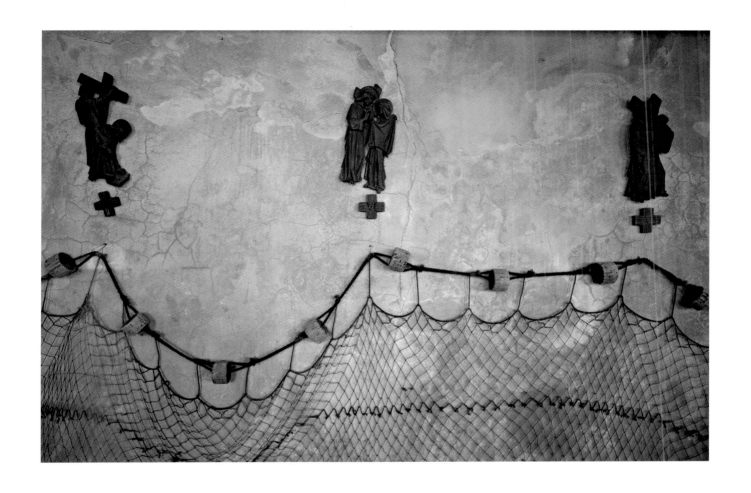

Holy Trinity and All Saints, Winterton, Norfolk

South Lochs, Isle of Lewis

Seal watch, Horsey, Norfolk

Walsingham, Whitsuntide, Norfolk

Brancaster Staithe, north Norfolk

St. Mary's, Great Walsingham, Norfolk

Whitsuntide, Walsingham, Norfolk

...Years ago, I walked over the Golden Gate Bridge to Sausalito. There were signs all along the bridge's parapet, admonishing the potentially suicidal promenaders: 'WARNING, THE CONSEQUENCES OF JUMPING FROM THIS BRIDGE CAN BE FATAL AND TRAGIC'. I liked the 'tragic', which seemed to me to unite this very big object with my own life's absolute inconsequence in the greater scheme of things. The mild high I experienced – standing in the middle of the vast structure, the wind soughing through its high-tension cables, and looking out over the deep azure waters of the bay at Alcatraz – soon dissipated as I trudged on into Sausalito. The roadway became low-slung and prosaic; the cars swishing past were embodied entirely in their own branding – their functionality subsumed entirely to marketing: to drive was to consume... Along the sidewalk, either side of a low seawall, there were piles of flat blue-grey stones – some only a few inches high, others over three feet. The stones had been artfully arranged, and indeed some of the artful arrangers were still at it: on their hands and knees, hair hooked behind ears, hands all a-tremor as they placed another stone on to their edifice, willing it to remain upright.

Others who'd walked across the bridge from San Francisco stopped to chat with the stone-pilers and admire their handiwork — I ignored them and strolled on. It pulled me back, this spectacle of makeshift creativity, to the winter I spent living in a remote house in the Orkney Islands. Orkney is largely formed by red sandstone, which, under erosive conditions of sea and wind fractures into

a complex joinery; the foreshores present a tumbledown aspect, and if you squint it becomes ambiguous: is this the rubble left behind by the collapse of ancient buildings, or is it only the continuous redevelopment of the earth's very crust? The invitation to join in whichever process it was could not be refused: in the afternoons, when I'd completed my allotted word-count for that day, I would scramble slowly over the rocks, picking out ones that caught my eye – by virtue of size, shape, colour and feel, rather than obvious utility – and pile them up, just as the dippy old hippies did along the road to Sausalito.

I knew what they were doing – because I knew what I'd been doing. Man's interventions in the natural world have acquired a scale and intensity that overpowers us – this was certainly the case by 1937 when the Golden Gate Bridge was completed; and even more compellingly so eight years later when Little Boy gave birth to the age of mega-death. It may well be that we experience the world as overpoweringly anthropocentric because we, of course, are anthropods – but that doesn't stop it being the case. Conscious of our own withered biophilia, and of our inability to apprehend reality as our fellow animals do, we have recourse to behaviours that mimic theirs: we construct nests, pile up mounds and build heaps. We do it with scant attention – or, rather, the sort of attention we bring to these pastimes is unfocussed and oneiric: we look for certain things, without any clear idea of what they might be; and when we arrange them, we hope to discover a patterning that's the product of forces operating beyond our conscious control: our castles align themselves on the

Smoked herring at HS Fishing, Great Yarmouth, Norfolk

beach, forming a futile defence against entropy, because it is itself… entropic.

When I've found myself in acute psychic distress, I've also found myself on traffic islands – sitting down on traffic islands with a collection of locally-sourced detritus – discarded lolly sticks, windblown twigs, the shards of plastic and metal trim cars moult – piled between my outstretched legs. I take a twig or a bit, I place it; I take another, I place that. I don't feel better – but this ordering of the material world is, I feel, preventing it from getting any worse. Edmund Husserl, the founder of the school of twentieth century philosophy called Phenomenology coined a hortatory slogan to express the essence of his approach: 'Back to the things themselves!' By 'things' he was referring to those mental objects which are presented directly to us in consciousness, for their nature is what he wished to investigate. The commonsense view is that the traffic island presented to us in consciousness corresponds – albeit not precisely – to a traffic island in 'the real world', but all humans are natural sceptics (we cannot prevent ourselves so being), and we can't stop ourselves from entertaining the possibility these things are known to us alone. Husserl took a term from ancient Greek philosophy – epoché, or 'suspension' – to characterise the nature of phenomenological enquiry. He felt it was only once we had 'bracketed' and set to one side any of our assumptions about the existence or otherwise of the external world, that we could begin to truly get back to the things themselves.

And these things we get back to are so invested with pathos — where does it come from? The poet, Theodor Roethke, writes of: 'The unalterable pathos of basin and pitcher, / Ritual of multigraph, paper-clip, comma, / Endless duplication of lives and objects.' It follows, surely, that in our arrangement of these dolorous things we become both philosophers — and gods. We suspend and bracket them on shelves, in nooks, and stacked up in sheds; we range them along sea walls and dangle them from trees; we create shrines to the departed, known and unknown; we arrange our tools before the day's work begins, and in the evenings, eating our solitary suppers, we make sure before we commence that knife and fork are still aligned with plate and glass. Each assemblage is itself a created world – while we're the deity who's immanent. We need this: the establishment of a zone within which faith works in order to sustain us as we wander through a wider world thronged by shades, revenants and ghosts. In the Northern and Western isles of Scotland these psychic middens are more salient in the landscape than the current inhabitants' dwellings: I recall walking up from the jetty of Papa Westray in Orkney and sensing the endless duplication of lives and objects in the ruined cottages beside the loch of St Tredwell. At the time I was thinking of the grisly legend: how Tredwell (or Triduana) was sent on a mission to the Pictish King Nechtan; how he fell in love with her and praised her beautiful eyes; and how, lest she succumbed to the vanity such flattery might provoke, she then plucked out those eyes, skewered them on a twig, and sent this grisly assemblage to the lovelorn monarch.

St Faith's, Little Witchingham, Norfolk

I recall entering one of the ruined cottages and finding amongst the rubble a slew of old knitting patterns dating from the 1950s; their faded images of dapper pipe-smokers in cardigans and Fair Isle woollies were as much of a memento mori as the arrangement of eyes and twigs that sanctified Triduana. It is the cosmic solecism of a secular age to imagine sacred arrangements cannot be material ones quite as much as the reverse: in the 1970s we collectively and unconsciously valorised the passing of an era in which the generality were engaged in meaningfully productive labour — we did it by making bookcases out of bricks and planks, or beds out of pallets and futons. All technology begins and ends not with innovation – but with faith; as Levi-Strauss observes in *The Savage Mind*, traditional peoples employ sympathetic magic not because they are credulous and superstitious (we are all credulous and superstitious), but because *it works*. We begin with an arbitrary selection of objects – but their arrangement is always painstaking. We no longer feel the presence in copse, thicket and osier bed of the psyches that once thronged the land. We no longer look out to sea and imagine the labour of those who harvest it. Instead manual labour has become at once historicised and irrelevant – another profit centre for the leisure industry. In the age of sail, seamen who had been without sight of land for too long sometimes developed a delirium known as calenture, wherein they believed the waves surrounding them were the rise and fall of their native rolling down land. Unless restrained, those afflicted might well step over the taffrail and stroll away to rendezvous with Davy Jones. It sometimes strikes me that we may

have reversed this disease-process in our own era: we've been away from the natural world for so long – staggering across concrete seas, caught in tarmac whirlpools – that when we see a passing car we mistake it for a horse and try to mount it.

Piles of hessian sacks; stacks of flattened cardboard boxes – rooms replete with ropes. The slow silent sifting of plaster dust through sunbeams – the coyly blank stare of a chipped gold-painted plaster cherub. It may be that religious ritual affords us this much: the only meaningful interaction with things that we still possess, for our own labour – by and large – contributes so little to what actually sustains us. By connecting with the threefold nature of the Godhead, or participating in the miracle of transubstantiation, we may hope to conjure up a realm of genuine materiality, one with pewter skies and a sun of molten brass – yet it's a forlorn hope: the solidity of the world we have lost ever-collapses back into this two-dimensional and papery reverence. Still, we cannot prevent ourselves from collecting the jam jars, washing them out and lining them up on our mantelpieces and windowsills, we can't stop the old tobacco tins from clanking in the shed – in old pre-Reformation churches a small internal window, called a hagioscope, might be inserted in the reredos, so worshippers could focus directly on the altar, or possibly an image or statue of a saint. This ritualised form of seeing and attendant contemplation belonged to a prelapsarian world – since Luther arranged his hammer and his nails, prior to posting up his epochal theses we've felt ourselves to be

Lionacleit, Benbecula, Western Isles

predestined (or perhaps condemned) to things.

Rusty metal and net curtaining; defunct stair rods and dented plastic barrels; the shells of razor clams and old wire-rimmed spectacles; a pottery souvenir of Dolgellau and a ball of Blu-Tack – our world is full up with itself, altogether replete. Our aim cannot be to produce yet more things, but only to arrange those we find lying around. In Jorge-Luis Borges's short story *Tlon Uqbar Orbis Tertius*, a secret society works for centuries to create the encyclopaedia of an imaginary universe; one in which all people are idealists rather than realists, so their commonsense view is that material objects which persist in space and time are… myths. They term these so-called 'things' *hronir*, and the revelation one has been seen is akin to someone in our world saying they witnessed a ghostly manifestation. Many interpretations can be placed on Borges's alternative universe, but I think the true one lies in the story's coda: the secret of Tlon has become known to the general public and begun to influence it – moreover, certain objects have begun to infiltrate our world; the story's unnamed narrator has a strange encounter with a ragged and deranged man in a remote inn:

> 'By daybreak, the man was dead in the hallway. The roughness of his voice had deceived us: he was only a youth. In his delirium a few coins had fallen from his belt, along with a cone of bright metal, the size of a die. In vain a boy tried to pick up this cone. A man was scarcely able to raise it from the ground. It held in my hand for a few minutes; I remember that its weight was intolerable and that after it was removed, the feeling of oppressiveness remained. I also remember the exact circle it pressed into my palm. The sensation of a very small and at the same time extremely heavy object produced a disagreeable impression of repugnance and fear.'

The disagreeable sensation of repugnance and fear is ours to savour: as we retreat from the physical realm into the virtual one we leave this disturbing wrack lying along the foreshore of our collective consciousness: We have nothing to do with things anymore – nothing productive that is; and we have nothing to do with God or gods anymore either; and so, for all our frenzied manipulations, the effects, henceforth, will be minimal, while the feeling of oppressiveness will remain – the same feeling that bore down on me as I trudged the weary road into Sausalito.

Will Self, London, 2015

THE CARVING
ON THESE STEPS
WAS GIVEN

BY THE CHILDREN
OF ALL SAINTS
1906.

FOOD BANK

All Saints, Thornham, Norfolk

South Uist, Western Isles

Stornoway Harbour, Isle of Lewis

Wherry Yacht Charter, Wroxham, Norfolk

Free Church (continuing), Scalpay, Isle of Harris

Brancaster, north Norfolk coast

Bhaltos, Isle of Lewis

Walsingham shop, Norfolk

Stefan Davies, photographer, Caolas Scalpaigh, Isle of Harris

John MacAulay's workshop, Flodabay, South Harris

Free Presbyterian church, Stokinish, South Harris

Scalpay, Isle of Harris

The Dolphin Inn, old fish wharf, Great Yarmouth, Norfolk

Hunstanton, Norfolk

Our Lady of the Waves and St. John, Vatersay, Western Isles

All Saints, Chedgrave, Norfolk

St. Mary's, North Creake, Norfolk

St. Margaret's, Cley, Norfolk

Hallway, Scalpay, Isle of Harris

St. Margaret's, Tatterford, Norfolk

South Uist, Western Isles

Our Lady of the Waves and St. John, Vatersay, Western Isles

St. Margaret's, Hardley, Norfolk Broads

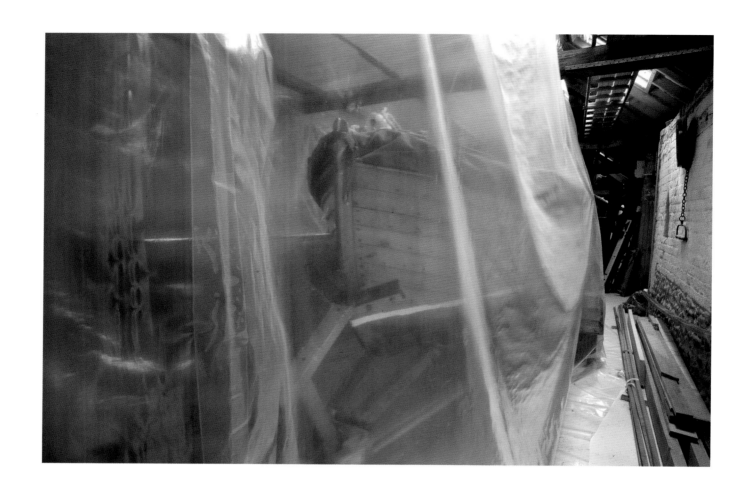

Ian Duffill's workshop, Thurning, Norfolk

All Saints, Swanton Morley, Norfolk

Sea bass, Brancaster, north Norfolk coast

Lake Lothing, Lowestoft, Suffolk

Net Services factory, Scalpay, Isle of Harris

Gill net fishing, Brancaster, Norfolk coast

Acknowledgements

Without Gus Wylie, my self-appointed mentor for *Affinity and Kindred*, you would not be reading this book. Gus has published four books of work from the Hebrides, is a long respected practitioner of documentary photography and has been unfailingly generous to me with his time and advice. In 1971, when Gus met the American photographer Paul Strand at London's ICA, they talked about Strand's Hebridean experiences resulting in his renowned book *Tir a' Mhurain* (1962). Despite the need for Gus to differentiate his work from Strand's collection and in turn for me to separate myself from Gus' oeuvre, this is the photographic legacy I have inherited and I delight in the continuity.

I am also indebted to Mike and Fiona Coulthard who invited me and my wife to stay with them on Scalpay in 2012; Roddy and June Johnstone for providing a welcoming and unexpected halfway house in Bannovie near Fort William, a perfect example of the kindness of strangers when our car broke down; Carla Macvicar, her brother Chris and his wife Marion who answered my advert in *De Tha Dol?*, the Harris Community Newsletter, and provided the billet which became 'Richard's Room' at their home in Tarbert, and to the Revds Kenneth MacDonald and Andrew Coghill on Scalpay for providing a genial introduction to the island community. Along the road in Scotland my thanks to Stefan Davies, Euan and Erica Galbraith, Morag McLeod, Tom Hayes, Sheila Roderick, Calum MacSween, Mossy MacKay, Alistair McLeod, Donald Hodgson, John Randle, Ewan Morrison, Steve Dilworth, Kate Macleod, John MacAulay, Donald and Rachel MacSween, Willie Fulton, John Morrison and Brillo and Ivor at Cuddy Point, Abdul and Alyas Ghaffar, Peter Dillistone, and Cathy Macleod, Maryann Ferguson and Claire Logan in Barra. South of the border many thanks for invaluable advice and support from Mark Cocker, Ian Duffill, Harry Malt, Sarah Knights, Ned Catt, Keith Launchbury, Robert Macfarlane, Amanda Geitner, Adrian Hodge, Peter Bower, Henry Fillery, Ken Tidd, Amanda Hopkinson, Neil Thompson, David Hewitt, Andy Wilson, Simon Middleton, Andrew Cowan, Joe Geitner, Bill Jackson, Chris Gribble, Writer's Centre Norwich, David Matless, Will Self and Phil Gray.

Finally, unconditional love and thanks to my wife and co-conspirator Caroline, and to the unreserved support of my brilliant and *au courant* sprogs, Madeleine and Oscar.

RD, Norfolk 2015

Notes to the photographs

Frontispiece: Hamarsaigh – off the edge of Scalpay, Isle of Harris, with the Cuillin mountains on the Isle of Skye in the background.

Page 2: Our Lady St Mary, South Creake, Norfolk

3: International Boatbuilding Training College, Lowestoft, Suffolk www.ibtc.co.uk.

4: Calum MacSween, Ardinashaig, Scalpay. Amongst many other practical skills, Calum is an accomplished stone wall builder. He is also Clerk to the Deacon's Court at Scalpay Free Church of Scotland (continuing).

5: Ken Tidd digs for lugworms on north Norfolk beaches. Ken is also an artist whose paintings appear regularly in Norfolk galleries.

6: Hushinish Beach, West Harris.

7: Dry stone walling by Calum MacSween.

8-9: Wassail procession, Elsing, Norfolk. This ancient custom is being re-imagined for the 21st century in a village close to where I live. In the cider-producing counties of South West and South East England and now the Eastern region, wassailing refers to a traditional ceremony that involves singing and drinking the health of trees on Twelfth Night in the hope that they might better thrive. The purpose of wassailing is to awaken the cider apple trees and to scare away evil spirits to ensure a good harvest of fruit in the autumn. Evil spirits hate a fiery procession as much as the locals enjoy one.

10: Organ pipes, St Margaret's, Tatterford, Norfolk

11: David Hewitt's boat yard, Stiffkey, Norfolk.

12: Tom Gathercole and David Hewitt, Hewitt's Boatyard, Stiffkey, north Norfolk.

13: Rachel and Donald MacSween, Scalpay, Isle of Harris. I discovered Rachel and Donald in the pages of Adam Nicholson's remarkable book *Sea Room*, the story of Nicholson's ownership of the Shiant Islands in the Minch. Donald used to tend a flock of sheep on the Shiants - he is described by Nicholson as 'a man of great propriety'. Rachel has a mischievous twinkle in her eye as she stops everything and prepares tea and cakes for callers.

14: Empty Church, South Uist.

15: Weybourne beach, north Norfolk. These two pictures remind me of the title of Tom Atkinson's guidebook to the west of Scotland, *The Empty Lands* (Luath Press 1986.)

16-17: You have to cross the Minch to get to the islands, whatever the weather. It is believed to be the site of the biggest meteorite ever to hit the British Isles. Sometimes it feels like another is on its way. This picture was actually taken just around the corner from north east Skye.

18: Neil Thompson's boat yard at Glandford, Norfolk. Neil's yard is the home of the Norfolk Range of boats, including the Norfolk Gypsy, a wood and glass fibre 20' yacht. http://www.neilthompsonboats.co.uk

19: Our Lady St Mary, South Creake, Norfolk.

20: Storage area at Henry Fillery's boat yard, Coldham Hall, Norfolk Broads.

21: Storage at an un-named church, Norfolk.

22: Our Lady of Sorrows Roman Catholic Church, Garryna-monie, South Uist - a spectacular Modernist building on the road down to Eriskay.

23: David Hewitt's boatyard, Stiffkey, Norfolk. http://www.norfolkboatbuilders.co.uk

24-25: A Scalpay croft.

26: Storage room at Wherry Yacht Charter, Wroxham, Norfolk Broads. Wherries used to proliferate in Broadland, carrying staple goods as well as passengers around the lakes and rivers. Now there are less than ten on the water mainly for visitors' pleasure and staffed by enthusiasts. Wherry Yacht Charter is at: http://www.wherryyachtcharter.org

27: A shop in the pilgrimage village of Walsingham, north Norfolk. You could possibly emerge with a completely equipped, staffed and functioning church.

28: Brillo and Ivor in the control room, Marine Harvest Salmon Farm, East Loch Tarbert. Feeding the salmon and managing the huge fish pens is all computer controlled. Each circular pen contains around 50,000 fish, which can be observed writhing via closed circuit cameras.

29: Melody and Estelle cleaning and sorting mussels, Brancaster, north Norfolk coast.

30: Net Services plant room, Scalpay, Harris. The factory used to be part of the salmon industry and is now a cleaning and servicing business for deep sea fishing nets.

31: The Anglican shrine of Our Lady of Walsingham, north Norfolk. According to Walsingham legend, in 1061 a Saxon noblewoman, Richeldis de Faverches, had a vision of the Virgin Mary in which she was instructed to build a replica of the house of the Holy Family in Nazareth in honour of the Annunciation. The village remains a major pilgrimage centre to this day.

32-33: St Nicholas, Salthouse, north Norfolk. In England's 1000 Best Churches, Penguin 1999, Simon Jenkins suggests that it is 'in every sense a lighthouse…When the Norfolk magnate Sir Henry Heydon rebuilt the church at the turn of the 16th century, he put it as high as he could, to be safe from floods and to act as a lantern for ships at sea.'

34: St Mary the Virgin, Titchwell, north Norfolk coast.

35: The workshop just outside Castlebay in Barra, where a group of local rowing enthusiasts constructed a St Ayles Skiff. www.jordanboats.co.uk/JB/stayles.htm

36: Steve Dilworth, sculptor, Geocrab, South Harris. On being asked for proof that one of his throwing objects really did contain a bird, Steve replied "destroy it and see". www.stevedilworth.com/home.htm

37: Donald MacSween, Scalpay.

38: A herring gutting shed slowly deflates on the harbour side in Scalpay, Isle of Harris – a vestige of the once massive herring industry.

39: A new crab boat, The Auk, takes shape at David Hewitt's boat yard in Stiffkey, north Norfolk coast. It is the first wooden crab boat to be built since 1989.

40-41: I was taken out to the Marine Harvest Salmon Farm operations barge on a choppy sea in East Loch Tarbert. The staff quarters' décor is straight from the 1960s. *"We've been expecting you Mr Bond…"*

42: David Hewitt's boat yard, Stiffkey, Norfolk.

43: Photographs of previous incumbents in St Margaret's, Cley, on the north Norfolk coast are also a record of the history of the medium and of formal portrait styles.

44: Bell ropes and change-ringing instructions, St Mary the Virgin, Elsing, Norfolk.

45: International Boatbuilding Training College, Lowestoft, Suffolk. http://www.ibtc.co.uk

46: Harvest time at Hewitt's yard, Stiffkey, Norfolk

47: Deacon's Court, Scalpay Free Church, October 2014. Left to right: Murdo MacSween, Angus Macleod, John Angus Macleod, Ewan Macleod, Andrew Coghill, Roddy Mackenzie, Donald John MacSween, Norman Morrison

48-49: The Clisham, Island of Harris. At 799 metres it is the highest mountain in the Outer Hebrides.

50: Net Services, Scalpay, Harris.

51: Free Presbyterian Church, Stokinish, South Harris

52: Priory Church of All Saints, Weybourne, north Norfolk

53: Ian Duffill supervised the building of the first St Ayles Skiff in Norfolk, *Hoi Larntan*, working with members of the local sailing and rowing community.

54: The view from the bedroom of my first rented billet on Scalpay, as I began this project in 2012.

55: St Michael's Roman Catholic Church, Eriskay, Western Isles

56-57: St Margaret's church, Cley, north Norfolk.

58: St Michael's Roman Catholic Church, Eriskay, Western Isles. The altar rests on the bow of a lifeboat washed overboard from the US aircraft carrier Hermes. Eriskay is the real *Whisky Galore* island.

59: Workbench at the International Boatbuilding Training College in Lowestoft, Suffolk. My eye was drawn by the Bible illustration pinned to the bench. I worked out that it depicts Noah warning a cynical crowd that a huge flood is about to devastate the world.

60: Vestry at St John's, Stiffkey, north Norfolk.

61: Vestry and Confessionals area at St Joseph's Roman Catholic Church, Howbeg, South Uist.

62: Hemsby, Norfolk coast.

63: The walls of Holy Trinity and All Saints at Winterton on the east Norfolk coast are decorated with nets and other fishing apparatus. A former rector, the committed Anglo-Catholic, Fr. Clarence Albert Pratt Porter, endeared himself to the people of the village, and was especially mindful of the lads and men of the drifters who followed the herring shoals around the country away up to Scotland and beyond. Fr Porter died tragically in 1932 after saving a young choir-boy from the sea. (Thanks to notes compiled by Fr Adrian Ling, Rector of Winterton.)

64-65: I'm not the first visitor to exclaim at the Mars-like landscapes of the Isle of Lewis – this one in the South Lochs area.

66: Seal watch, Horsey Beach, Norfolk. Hundreds of grey seals breed in this area and can be viewed during the winter months.

67: Clerics gather at the Whitsuntide pilgrimage in Walsingham, north Norfolk.

68: Fishing nets at Brancaster Staithe, north Norfolk.

69: Plastic sheets protect the altar during repair work at St Mary's, Great Witchingham, Norfolk.

70: Assorted clerics at Walsingham, Whitsuntide.

72: Smoked herring at HS Fishing, Great Yarmouth. In 1913, there were over 10,000 boats involved in the herring industry. Many of the workers were Scottish women – fisher lasses – who travelled between the Hebrides and Norfolk filleting and packing. The industry ended during the late 1960s. John Grierson's 1929 film 'Drifters', is a brilliant evocation of the life and times of workers and fleets around the Scottish and English coast.

74: St Faith's, Little Witchingham, Norfolk

76: Lionacleit, Benbecula, Western Isles

78: Sign of the times in All Saints, Thornham, north west Norfolk.

79: Roadside shrine, South Uist, Western Isles.

80: On the slipway, Stornoway Harbour, Isle of Lewis.

81: Wherry Yacht Charter, Wroxham, Norfolk. www.wherryyachtcharter.org

82: Free Church (continuing), Scalpay, Harris

83: Oyster holding store, Brancaster, north Norfolk coast

84-85: Bhaltos, Isle of Lewis. Most cemeteries on the islands are located on the western seaboard where there is deeper earth. Processions are often seen traveling across from funeral services in churches in rockier eastern districts.

86: Shop window, Walsingham, north Norfolk

87: Stefan presents and sells striking views of Hebridean land and seascapes in his small roadside gallery near the bridge to Scalpay. www.harrishebridesphotos.co.uk/caolasgallery.php

88: John MacAulay's workshop, Flodabay, South Harris. … John is the remaining traditional wooden boat builder in the Western Isles. He says *'there is only one boat worth having and that is a wooden boat. They are unique; one off and beautiful. How anyone with any sensitivity could choose a plastic hull over a wooden one made by hand, I will never know'*.

89: Free Presbyterian Church, Stokinish, South Harris.

90: Scalpay, Isle of Harris.

91: The Dolphin Inn, old fish wharf, Great Yarmouth. More vestiges of the herring industry referred to elsewhere.

92-93: Hunstanton, north Norfolk.

94: Our Lady of the Waves and St John, Vatersay, Western Isles.

95: St Margaret's, Hardley, Norfolk Broads.

96: Homemade jam for sale at St Mary's, North Creake, Norfolk.

97: St Margaret's, Cley, north Norfolk. There is a gendered subtext to many of the photographs in this book – mainly male. From my own background the assumption is made (!) that women are responsible for flowers and cloths (altar and cleaning) in churches. This also applies to jam (and tea) making and many other essentially domestic roles.

98: A fisherman's hallway, Scalpay, Isle of Harris.

99: Vesting area, St Margaret's, Tatterford, Norfolk. These two photographs in particular repay detailed study.

100-101: South Uist, Western Isles.

102: Our Lady of the Waves and St John, Vatersay, Western Isles.

103: All Saints, Chedgrave, Norfolk. A curious visual echo discovered many months after each picture was made.

104: Ian Duffill's workshop, Thurning, Norfolk

105: All Saints, Swanton Morley, Norfolk.

106: Gill net-caught sea bass at Brancaster, north Norfolk coast.

107: Beside Lake Lothing, Lowestoft, Suffolk.

108: Net Services, Scalpay, Harris.

109: Gill net fishing, Brancaster, north Norfolk coast.

'He explained the sociology of boat construction, the importance of having neighbourly or kindred materials next to each other… I thought of how for Ian, objects and materials, like people and language, all had their fitness for purpose verified by use.'

Robert Macfarlane, *The Old Ways* p.114/115 (Hamish Hamilton 2012).